GW00455810

SO, WHAT HAPPENED?

by

Jennie Papa

So, What Happened?
Copyright © 2022 by Jennie Papa
ISBN:9798799731588

All rights reserved. No part of this publication may be
reproduced or transmitted in any form or by any means
without written permission from the author.

Scriptures taken from the Holy Bible, New International
Version®, NIV®. Copyright © 1973, 1978, 1984, 2011 by
Biblica, Inc.™ Used by permission of Zondervan. All rights
reserved worldwide. www.zondervan.com The "NIV" and
"New International Version" are trademarks registered in the
United States Patent and Trademark Office by Biblica, Inc.™

Scripture quotations marked (TPT) are from The Passion
Translation®. Copyright © 2017, 2018, 2020 by Passion &
Fire Ministries, Inc. Used by permission. All rights
reserved. ThePassionTranslation.com

Scripture quotations marked (TLB) are from The Living Bible
copyright © 1971. Used by permission of Tyndale House
Publishers, Carol Stream, Illinois 60188. All rights reserved.

Scripture quotations marked (MSG) are taken from THE
MESSAGE, copyright © 1993, 2002, 2018 by Eugene H.
Peterson. Used by permission of NavPress, represented by
Tyndale House Publishers. All rights reserved.

Scripture quotations marked (NKJV) are taken from the New
King James Version®. Copyright © 1982 by Thomas Nelson.
Used by permission. All rights reserved.

Quote by Dr Mark Batterson used by permission of National
Community Church, Washington, DC. All rights reserved.

In the beginning God created the
heavens and the earth.

(Genesis 1:1)

He who testifies to these things says,
"Yes, I am coming soon." Amen. Come, Lord Jesus.
The grace of the Lord Jesus be
with God's people Amen.

(Revelation 22:20-21)

SO, WHAT HAPPENED?

CHRISTIANITY EXPLAINED FOR BEGINNERS
AND THOSE SEEKING DEEPER
UNDERSTANDING OF THE BORN-AGAIN
EXPERIENCE...it helps us to grasp how the
Kingdom of God works and how we fit into it

Unpack the Framework and Outline of your
Spiritual Journey into Christianity

CONTENTS

FOREWORD

From Benny & Lynda Ojiakor – Wisdom of Faith Ministries

We have known Jennie for a number of years as a faithful Bible Teacher. She is an instructor on our Faith for Purpose Programme, which is aimed at empowering individuals to find and fulfil their inherent life purpose.

We are so glad that Jennie was obedient to write this book. It is a straight to the point work! It's written with such simplicity and clarity that we could find ourselves reading it over and over again as a refresher. This book gives clear insight to people who are new in the Christian faith; what happens during the experience of coming into faith; and for those who want a deeper understanding of a living relationship with Jesus Christ.

In our opinion, there are not many books out there that address this subject as this. This is so needed!

Wisdom of Faith Ministries – My Inherent Life Purpose Matters
For more information on our training and events please visit: www.wisdomoffaithministies.com

ACKNOWLEDGEMENTS

This book would never have been written without the prompting of friends and their encouragement and support. My thanks go to all those along the way who have, either knowingly or unknowingly, contributed to my development, both as a Christian and as a teacher.

My special thanks go to Rita, who doggedly urged me forward to share my own learning with others, and has contributed her own artistic skills in the cover and with producing my ichthus logo displayed in this book. Where would we be without those along our way to help, support and urge us on to better and higher goals.

My overall thanks go to God Himself, for it is He who has grounded me in His Word and revealed to me His story.

INTRODUCTION

It was never my intention to put my discoveries in the Word of God down on paper in this way – in fact it was the last thing on my mind. However, a number of years ago, Bruce, a friend of mine, said in passing that I should write a book. At the time I dismissed it from my thinking, but in more recent times another friend, Rita, has also said I should write a book, and gone on to mention it not once, but on several occasions. This made me take the suggestion seriously. I brought it before the Lord and He seemed to encourage the idea, so I set about the task.

I don't know about you, but I find it helps me to receive the revelation of a thing if I understand its purpose, and how and why it works. Like marriage, parenthood, a new job, etc., until we are actually doing it, we don't quite know what to expect. We know quite a bit, have heard things and read much. It is the same with walking with God. This book is aimed at people who are new in the Christian faith, but also for those who want more of a deeper under-standing of what happened during the experience of coming into faith. Given this, I have set out to be as clear as possible, and as simple as possible, whilst covering all the essential truths.

Maybe you haven't yet entered the Christian fold; maybe you have heard a lot about it, have become interested to know more, and maybe you are reading this book to gain understanding as to what it is about before you take the plunge. I believe you will find answers here, and I look forward to travelling this road with you.

So, What Happened? is a look at aspects of my journey with God through life, and what I have found out along the way with regard to the subjects covered in this publication. Your journey will be different from mine; your experiences different from mine; but you will see links and similarities, and I believe what you read here will help you to better understand your own journey with God. This is not an exhaustive work on these subjects, but is aimed at giving the reader a starting place.

Like everyone, I have made mistakes along the way and learnt the hard way often, but my aim was to do things God's way and to change. We don't see the changes unless and until they become bigger in our lives, but others see them in us. Change in line with God's Word should be our aim in life. His book, the Bible, is our manual for life, health and godliness.

The initial events and steps in our Christian walk are my focus in this book. I have tried to lay them out so you can understand what happens when you believe God's Word and take a leap of faith into the unknown. My hope is that my spiritual journey will help you with your own.

Unless otherwise stated, the Bible passages used here to illustrate each point are from the New International Version, and I have listed the name of the book, followed by the chapter and verse, e.g. Genesis 1:1. Where other versions are used, I have added the initials for that version in brackets. Further information on the various versions used can be found in the credits given on the permissions page at the front of this book. Words with capital letters you might not have been expecting, like Lord, Word, He, His, etc., all refer to God himself. Where I have quoted other people, the name of the author is acknowledged in the text. I encourage you to do your own study and receive your own revelation.

> [11]Now the Berean Jews were of more noble character than those in Thessalonica, for they received the message with great eagerness and examined the Scriptures every day to see if what Paul said was true. (Acts 17:11)

Here we see the Berean Jews checking out what Saint Paul told them. We should do the same and be settled in our own minds as to what we believe.

If what I have written so far ticks your boxes, then read on...

PART 1

Chapter 1
The New You

I shall use the term *born-again* throughout this publication; but this experience can also be referred to by other names; for example, 'seeing the light', 'becoming a Christian', 'making a commitment'; and these are just different terms for the same experience of coming into relationship with our Heavenly Father, through Jesus Christ. But what happened at that moment? My aim in this section is to explain this.

GOD IS A FAMILY GUY

The Bible tells us that when we are born-again the Father receives us through Jesus and adopts us into His family as sons. A word to the ladies reading this book – you too are sons when you become born-again. Why should this be? At the time the Bible was written, and for a long time after, it was the sons who inherited from their fathers, and they were also given place and responsibility in the family. Your Heavenly Father will not deny you your inheritance in Him, or your call to be a part of His Kingdom ministry – therefore, it's ok to be content with being a son.

Take a look at the following:

> *³If you belong to Christ, then you are Abraham's seed, and heirs according to the promise. (Galatians 3:29)*
>
> *⁶This mystery is that through the gospel the Gentiles are heirs together with Israel, members together of one body, and sharers together in the promise in Christ Jesus. (Ephesians 3:6)*
>
> *⁷...so that, having been justified by his grace, we might become heirs having the hope of eternal life. (Titus 3:7)*

So we see that by being born-again we become sons and heirs. Why has it been necessary for God to do it this way? For an answer to this question, we need to go back to the very beginning.

The word 'Genesis' means *the origin or coming into being*

of something, and the first book of the Bible – Genesis – tells us how God put everything together.

IN THE BEGINNING

If you want to read about how God created the heavens, the earth, and everything in them, from day to day during the creation period, you can find this account in Genesis 1:1-25. We will be looking at what happened immediately after creation.

We know from other verses of the Bible that God is one God but manifested in three persons – Father, Son and Holy Spirit – each with His own unique part to play; these three are sometimes referred to as the Trinity or the Godhead.

In verses 26-27 of Genesis chapter 1, we see the Godhead discussing creating man to be made in God's own image and likeness, (that is, the species of mankind, both male and female, in the form of Adam). Notice the use of the plural as the Trinity refer both to themselves (us and our), and as they speak of the man they will create (they and them).

> *[26]Then God said, "Let us make mankind in our image, in our likeness, so that they may rule over the fish in the sea and the birds in the sky, over the livestock and all the wild animals, and over all the creatures that move along the ground."*
> *[27]So God created mankind in his own image, in the*

image of God he created them; male and female
he created them. (Genesis 1:26-27)

Adam, made in the likeness of God, had similarities to his Heavenly Father. He could think like God, act like God. We know God has arms and legs; He has emotions; He can sing, dance, whistle, and more; all things we humans can do.

The part of Adam made in God's image was his spirit. God is a spirit being and, although you may not have thought about this, we, being made in His image, are also spirit beings, even though we have a body.

God made Adam out of the dust of the earth, and it is God who breathed life into him.

> *[7] Then the LORD God formed a man from the dust*
> *of the ground and breathed into his nostrils the*
> *breath of life, and the man became a living being.*
> *(Genesis 2:7)*

Being formed in the likeness of God means we too are three-part beings. We are made up of our spirit, our soul, and our body, and Adam fellowshipped with God through his spirit. We will look further into this later on.

So, having prepared the world, the universe, and everything else, God created Adam, and placed him into the Garden of Eden. Eden was created perfectly – with beautiful trees and plants, amazing scenery, the perfect temperature, an on-tap food supply. If we consider the wonders of today's world, which are indeed magnificent, how much more wonderful would it have been before Adam's sin tarnished it.

HERE FOR PURPOSE

While living and enjoying this environment, Adam met with God on a regular basis and they fellowshipped together. During this time God revealed to Adam his life's purpose.

He was to increase in number – just as God had created him in His likeness, with the same identity as God and the ability to think like God – so Adam should create others in his likeness.   In so doing, this increase would fill the earth. Adam was told to subdue the earth, bringing everything under his authority; that authority being given to him by his father, God. So we see that Adam was blessed, which meant he was equipped to succeed in all areas of life and godliness. Genesis goes on to say:

> *[28]God blessed them and said to them, "Be fruitful and increase in number; fill the earth and subdue it. Rule over the fish in the sea and the birds in the sky and over every living creature that moves on the ground." (Genesis 1:28)*

Once again, this is written using plural words when referring to mankind in the form of Adam.

A TALE OF TWO TREES

Another message God gave Adam was to tell him about a special tree in the middle of the Garden. God warned Adam that the fruit of this tree – *the tree of the knowledge of good and evil* – was not to be eaten.   All other trees were available to him for food, but not this one. If he ate its fruit, there would be consequences. Genesis 2 goes on to say:

> [16]*And the* LORD *God commanded the man, "You are free to eat from any tree in the garden;* [17]*but you must not eat from the tree of the knowledge of good and evil, for when you eat from it you will certainly die." (Genesis 2:16-17)*

The original Hebrew says it like this – *in dying you will die.* Why two *dyings?*

Remember Adam was made in the likeness and image of God, and thought like God, and could act like God. This first dying refers to Adam's spirit – if Adam disobeyed God and ate from the forbidden tree, although he would still be made in God's likeness, he would no longer be in the image of God. Disobedience would change things. His spirit would become dead to God.

When the words *dead* or *death* are mentioned in the Bible it does not mean ceasing to exist; it means being separated, away from God. Adam's dead spirit would become totally self-centered, and self-absorbed, and would no longer be in tune with the Father's Spirit. Consequently, Adam's relationship and closeness to his Father would be broken, due to his spirit (made in the image of God) dying. God is a spirit being, and Adam fellowshipped with Him through his spirit – spirit to Spirit. God and Adam would still be able to communicate with each other but would no longer have the closeness and intimacy that was originally experienced.

The second *dying* refers to Adam's body. Due to his connection to the Father (who is his source of life) becoming very different, his body would begin to deteriorate, eventually dying. At this point, however, Adam didn't know what death looked like as the earth was perfect, and he only had knowledge of the perfect and perfection.

Next to this forbidden tree, however, God placed *the tree of life*. Although God doesn't discuss this with Adam, the purpose of this other tree is to seal human beings into their perfect relationship with God should they choose to eat of it instead of *the tree of the knowledge of good and evil*. God always gives us choices in life – our job is to choose the right one.

Life continued for Adam on his own for a while but before too long God put Adam into a deep sleep and formed Eve. Let's take a look at how this was possible.

You will remember that in Genesis 1:27 we learnt that when God created mankind in Adam, He created them male and female. From this we discover that everything necessary to form Eve was already inside Adam. So when Adam slept, God removed from him the female part, making the one into two. This is why the Word of God discloses that when a man and woman marry, they become one flesh, thus bringing back the two into the oneness created by God.

This is also why divorce is so painful – it is like having your arm torn off, which leaves you hurting and less of a person than you were. Also notice, Eve came from Adam's side – not from his feet, that he would walk over her – nor from his head, that she would rule over him – but his side, because they were in partnership. Different parts of the same – with different tasks and functions.

Now we have two people – one flesh – both made in the likeness and image of God. These two will have spent their days together and, although it is not specifically mentioned in the Bible, Adam must have relayed to Eve all that God had told him in order to bring her up to speed. This will have included the message God gave Adam about the tree in the middle of the Garden.

SO WHAT WENT WRONG?

The day came when the two were in the vicinity of the tree with forbidden fruit, *the tree of the knowledge of good and evil.*

Now Satan was originally one of the top angels in God's Kingdom, and his name there was Lucifer. He is believed to have been in charge of the music, praise and worship in heaven. He enjoyed his position of authority. Now, suddenly, we have God forming a family with human beings. Angels are not family. They are servants of God. Family means a greater closeness, a greater intimacy, a greater connection with the Most High.

Satan wanted to be just like God; he wanted to rule and reign as if he was God. He desired the authority, which was given to Adam, for himself. These words are spoken by God about Satan.

> [13] *You said in your heart,*
> *"I will ascend to the heavens –*
> *I will raise my throne above the stars of God;*
> *I will sit enthroned on the mount of assembly,*
>   *on the utmost heights of Mount Zaphon*
> [14] *I will ascend above the tops of the clouds;*
> *I will make myself like the Most High."*
> *(Isaiah 14:13-14)*

So, with Adam and Eve near the forbidden tree, Satan saw his opportunity to take advantage of the situation to steal the authority that God had given Adam. He took up residence in a serpent, and started talking to Eve. Why did he choose her and not Adam?

You will probably have noticed that men and women are wired differently. The two sexes are two halves of the same coin – but different in form and function. Some of us like to chat, others not so much. I believe Eve liked to talk. As a woman I can say that my experience is that ladies do like to talk, and I feel she was engaged in conversation because:

(a)   she was a woman who liked to chat, and,

(b)   she hadn't been told directly by God not to eat the forbidden fruit; she received the information second-hand, so to speak, from Adam.

Let's take a look at Genesis chapter 3.

> *¹Now the serpent was more crafty than any of the wild animals the LORD God had made. He said to the woman, "Did God really say, 'You must not eat from any tree in the garden'?"*
>
> *²The woman said to the serpent, "We may eat fruit from the trees in the garden, ³but God did say, 'You must not eat fruit from the tree that is in the middle of the garden, and you must not touch it, or you will die.'"*
>
> *⁴"You will not certainly die," the serpent said to the woman. ⁵"For God knows that when you eat from it your eyes will be opened, and you will be like God, knowing good and evil."*
>
> *⁶When the woman saw that the fruit of the tree was good for food and pleasing to the eye, and also desirable for gaining wisdom, she took some and ate it. She also gave some to her husband, who was with her, and he ate it. ⁷Then the eyes of both of them were opened, and they realized they were naked; so they sewed fig leaves together and made coverings for themselves. (Genesis 3:1-7)*

In verse 1 the conversation begins. The serpent asked Eve, *did God really say?* Here we see Satan putting doubt in Eve's mind. Did God really say? When we are questioned along these lines ourselves, we tend to take a step back and reconsider before we answer, often concurring with the doubt.

In verses 2-3 Eve informed the serpent that they could eat from all the trees in the Garden, except this one. She went on to say however, that they mustn't touch it or they would die. Here we see Eve adds to what God has said *we must not touch it*. We know from Genesis 2:16-17 that God did not use these words.

Verses 4-5 show the serpent countering God's words telling Eve that she would not certainly die, but by eating she would have her eyes opened. She and Adam would become like God – of course this was a lie because both Adam and Eve were already made in the image and likeness of God. Satan also told them they would have the knowledge of good and evil. Up to this point neither Adam nor Eve knew what evil was. Maybe it sounded exciting or enticing, but they had never seen it. Here we learn that the message from the serpent was nearly correct, but had a lie at its heart. Yes, they would have the knowledge of good and evil (evil being a thing God never wanted us to experience or know about), but the serpent denied eating the fruit would bring death. He seemed to be saying that God had withheld something from them!

So with the doubt in her mind, and the words of the serpent countering what God had said (thus calling God a liar) she studied the fruit, and verse 6 tells us that the fruit looked delicious, promised knowledge they didn't have, would fill in any gaps God had left; so she took it and ate. Adam was by her side and she gave it to him to eat also, which he did.

> ^{3}...just as Eve was deceived by the serpent's cunning... (2 Corinthians 11:3)

> ^{12}When Adam sinned, sin entered the entire human race. His sin spread death throughout all the world, so everything began to grow old and die, for all sinned. (Romans 5:12) (TLB)

Now here's a question. We see from the above verses that it was Adam that sinned, and Eve was only deceived. Why was that? Well, Adam had the information about *the tree of the knowledge of good and evil* straight from God, Eve didn't; and Adam didn't speak up to correct the situation while Eve was chatting with Satan through the serpent. He just allowed the conversation to roll on, and became complicit in his response. That's why he sinned, and Eve was deceived.

So, what we have learnt so far is about the fall of man and our separation from God, how it happened, and the consequences attached to it. But that's not the end of the story...

NOT THE END OF THE STORY

Before God created any of the heavens, earth, universe; because He knew the end from the beginning, God had a plan to save us. Ephesians chapter 1 explains:

> ^{4}For he chose us in him before the creation of the world to be holy and blameless in his sight. In love he ^{5}predestined us for adoption to sonship

through Jesus Christ, in accordance with his pleasure and will. (Ephesians 1:4-5)

We see here that before the creation of the world God already knew how it would pan out with Adam and Eve, that the earth would enter a fallen state, and that mankind would lose its close relationship with Him through sin. It goes on to say that He made provision for people to be lifted from this fallen state and become holy and blameless before Him, thus enabling us to be adopted into His family as sons. This process is known as being *born-again*.

Why did God make this provision knowing beforehand what a mess we would get into? The answer may surprise you – He did this because He loves us, and also for His own pleasure. We give Him pleasure. Did you know that?

BORN-AGAIN

When Jesus was on earth He was often picked on by the Pharisees (the ruling Jewish religious body of the day). They followed Him around, heard what He preached and taught, and saw what He did. They didn't like it and found fault with it whenever they could, trying to place Jesus in a bad light legally (according to Jewish law). However, one of their number, a man named Nicodemus, had questions, and he needed answers. Because his fellow Pharisees would not have approved of his seeking out Jesus with his questions, Nicodemus went to Jesus at night. John chapter 3 gives the account:

¹Now there was a Pharisee, a man named Nicodemus who was a member of the Jewish ruling council. ²He came to Jesus at night and said, "Rabbi, we know that you are a teacher who has come from God. For no one could perform the signs you are doing if God were not with him."

³Jesus replied, "Very truly I tell you, no one can see the kingdom of God unless they are born again."

⁴"How can someone be born when they are old?" Nicodemus asked. "Surely they cannot enter a second time into their mother's womb to be born!"

⁵Jesus answered, "Very truly I tell you, no one can enter the kingdom of God unless they are born of water and the Spirit. ⁶Flesh gives birth to flesh, but the Spirit gives birth to spirit. ⁷You should not be surprised at my saying, 'You must be born again.'
(John 3:1-7)

Here we have a ruler in Israel coming to Jesus at night so that his visit remains secret from his colleagues, and he begins with the pleasantries of the day. We would greet someone and ask how they are, and maybe mention the weather or something like that. Here, Nicodemus greets Jesus with words explaining it is clearly seen he is a good man and from God. At this point Jesus, who has become aware of why Nicodemus has come to Him (and already knows the questions he wishes to ask because the Holy Spirit had revealed them to Him in an unseen way), jumps straight in with answers. All civilities cease and Jesus cuts straight to the chase. He speaks of being *born-again*, as discussed in the passage above.

Nicodemus seems perplexed by Jesus' statements and responds with more questions. What does He mean by being born-again; how is it possible? Does he need to re-enter his mother's womb?

Nicodemus is an elder of Israel, so is of mature age, and his mother may well be dead! Jesus presents His answer giving a natural picture to help Nicodemus understand this spiritual issue. However, Nicodemus is unable to grasp it. This needs to be understood on a spiritual level. To anyone who thinks naturally like Nicodemus, this doesn't make sense. Let's dig a bit deeper.

John chapter 3 goes on to explain. When we are born, we are born naturally, and babies in the womb are protected in a sac of water (amniotic fluid) until the moment of birth. Also, immediately before giving birth, a mother experiences her 'waters breaking', which is the release of the fluid showing the birth is imminent. Verse 5 speaks of being *born of water and the Spirit*. The *born of water* refers to the natural birth.

Remember, that originally we were made in the image and likeness of God? It was Adam's spirit that was made in God's image, and it was Adam's spirit that died with the fall into sin in the Garden of Eden, thus changing him, and from then on he was no longer made in God's image, only in His likeness. So we, as Adam's offspring, are also therefore no longer made in the image of God (though still in His likeness), but made in the image of the fallen Adam. This also applied to Eve as she was part of the episode with the serpent.

Verse 5 goes on to say that spiritual birth is having our dead spirit revived into life with God. So, being *born of water and the Spirit* means: *water* is the natural birth, and *the Spirit* brings spiritual birth. We all have the first – natural birth, but the second – spiritual birth, is something we decide for ourselves, whether we want it or not. God is a gentleman and has given us free will to make our own choices, and will not compel us to be born-again. We must make this choice for ourselves. No-one can make this decision for us.

When I was seeking spiritual truth prior to being born-again, I read some Christian books to help my understanding. One thing that stood out to me was the phrase *God has no grandchildren.* Whatever did that mean? It bothered me until I discovered the answer. It is you who can become a child of God through Jesus, with direct relationship to God as your Father. You cannot become part of God's family through anyone else – not through your parents, your spouse, or any other person. The decision to enter into God's family is yours alone.

DECISIONS, DECISIONS!

When I was growing up, and also as a young adult, I thought I was a Christian. After all, I lived in a Christian country, I believed what the Bible says, I went to church and was confirmed as a member of the Church of England, I prayed. Surely that meant I was a Christian and okay with God, didn't it? It had never been explained to me that a response was required of me.

Then the time came when I began questioning all this. I had moved home and joined a different church. This new church contained born-again Christians (whatever they were – I didn't know at the time), who spoke freely about their faith. So, just like Nicodemus had questions, I too had questions and needed answers.

Maybe you have reached this point and realised that you have yet to go through this born-again experience and have no idea how to achieve it. It's a simple matter, and I address this further on in this book. But in the meantime, let's look at what Romans says:

> *[9]If you declare with your mouth, "Jesus is Lord," and believe in your heart that God raised him from the dead, you will be saved. (Romans 10:9)*

You can see here that your heart and your mouth must be in agreement. Your just saying a prayer will not change anything. You need to have a real need within yourself (in your heart) and be prepared to speak that need out (with your mouth).

> *[45]A good man brings good things out of the good stored up in his heart, and an evil man brings evil*

*things out of the evil stored up in his heart. For the
mouth speaks what the heart is full of.   (Luke 6:45)*

If your heart is full of the desire to become part of God's
family, and you are actively pursuing this relationship, you
will find yourself also desiring to speak out that need
(maybe to other people, or maybe to God in prayer).   Of
course, if for any reason someone is unable to speak (for
example they could be mute), then God, who sees into our
hearts, will hear their deepest desires and accept them.

What is the criteria to be born-again?

- You need to believe in God

- You need to believe that God's Son Jesus, is Lord.

- You need to believe that God raised Him from the
  dead.

If you believe these things, or are open-minded about
them, or have questions like Nicodemus and me, then you
are on your way.

Chapter 2

Our Just Deserts?

I suspect that most, if not all of you reading this book, have heard people use the phase – you reap what you sow. It refers to our actions, our attitudes, the way we behave towards others, doing a full circle and coming back to us. Sometimes this can be a good thing. If we offer friendship or support in various ways for instance, these things come back to us, often multiplied. However, if we are mean spirited, stingy or cruel, these things also return to us, like a boomerang, and we are not so happy to receive the negative returns.

This idea comes straight from the Bible. In Galatians it says:

> *⁶Do not be deceived: God cannot be mocked. A man reaps what he sows. (Galatians 6:7)*

But, here's a question for you – when it comes to the subject of salvation – that is, being born-again – and what Jesus did for us on the cross (which is indeed considerable and which we will look at in another chapter), do we deserve what has been achieved?

The quick answer is an emphatic **no**. No matter who we are, what we have done or not done, there is no-one who deserves anything good from God, because we have all fallen below His standard.

> *³...for all have sinned and fall short of the glory of God, (Romans 3:23)*

I am sure you, like me, are aware of wrong things we have done, often regretting them. If what we do comes back to us, then we deserve nothing good because we are fallen creatures. So why then, if we deserve nothing, did Jesus come? He chose to leave heaven with all its glory; He chose to leave behind His majesty and power; He chose to come to earth as a human being, to live a lowly life among us; but why, when He didn't have to? He came because He loved us and considered us worth saving out of the mess we had made for ourselves.

God's love for His created children (that's you and me) was, and remains, so great, and He saw our need was so vast, He wanted to get involved. Take a look at John chapter 3.

> *¹⁶For God so loved the world that he gave his one and only Son, that whoever believes in him shall not perish but have eternal life. ¹⁷For God did not send his Son into the world to condemn the world, but to save the world through him. (John 3:16-17)*

So, we deserve nothing, but Jesus came to save us because He loves us and thinks we are worth saving.

BEFORE IT ALL BEGAN

Let's look again at Ephesians.

> *⁴For he chose us in him before the creation of the world to be holy and blameless in his sight. In love ⁵he predestined us for adoption to sonship through Jesus Christ, in accordance with his pleasure and will. (Ephesians 1:4-5)*

Here we discovered that before creation had taken place, God had already predestined to become part of His family, those who would have a heart for Him. He knew what a mess we would make of things and He knew the people who would respond to Him, and Jesus had already committed to coming to earth to redeem us out of our plight, and to reconcile us back to the Father.

Let's take a look at why it had to be done this way.

Back in the Garden of Eden, Adam and Eve made a choice to eat from the tree from which God had said they should not eat. They were disobedient. They chose their own way without consulting their Heavenly Father, and did it – *because it felt good!* I am sure you can identify with this, as I can – haven't we all done things contrary to what we should just for our own pleasure, or to get back at someone? You will remember that Adam's disobedience opened the door to death (separation from God).

So we see that Adam (a man) allowed this to happen. He couldn't have known the consequences of this, but is held accountable as he did nothing to stop it. The Bible tells us that he is responsible for opening this door.

> *[12]When Adam sinned, sin entered the entire human race. His sin spread death throughout all the world, so everything began to grow old and die, for all sinned. (Romans 5:12) (TLB)*

This act resulted in Adam being changed, and his allegiance to God as his Father now became transferred to Satan, because he succumbed to temptation and did as Satan suggested through the serpent, instead of following God's instruction to him.

Having been created with a godly nature, Adam's nature was now changed. He was no longer made in the image of God as his spirit had just died (become separated from God), and he and God could no longer fellowship together as they once had, because the intimacy was gone.

In the natural, we receive our nature from our parents, just as Adam had received his godly nature from his parent – his Heavenly Father. Once sin entered the world the nature of human beings was changed forever, because now we were receiving the nature of Adam through our parents, from generation to generation. When we are born into this world we receive a carnal nature – that is, a worldly, non-spiritual nature – through Adam. This is called *original sin*. None of us mere mortals can escape being born in this way. However, Jesus has come to our rescue.

A man (Adam) gave away the authority God had given him to rule and fill the earth and have dominion over it. God always keeps his Word. He had given the authority over the earth to Adam and those who came after him, and if He took it back, He would be breaking His own Word.

God never breaks His Word! So how would it ever be possible to take this authority back?

HOW IT WAS DONE

God's original world was perfect. It was glorious. There was nothing wrong with it. A man had given away the human race's right to authority over it, and it was a man that was needed to buy it back, but if every person born after Adam and Eve inherited Adam's carnal nature, who would ever be able to do this?

When the fall happened (the entry of sin into the world), people became more and more sinful as time passed. It was a downward spiral. Eventually God had to put in place some instructions in order to curb sin, or people would become nothing but completely evil. This He did by giving the Jewish law (the ten commandments) through Moses.

The purpose of the law was to show God's people that His standard is perfect and set so high that we, as fallen men and women, cannot reach it. God used it as a schoolmaster to teach and guide the people until Messiah Jesus came.

> *24The Jewish laws were our teacher and guide until Christ came to give us right standing with God through our faith. (Galatians 3:24) (TLB)*

God wanted men and women to see this and come to Him for mercy and help, understanding their inability to fulfil the law. An example of what I am speaking of here is – if I am not a good artist but believe I can paint a masterpiece, I am deluding myself.

Unfortunately, God's people missed the point (and subsequently some of the church also have) and they thought the law was a code for how to live. If they didn't commit murder, adultery, didn't steal, etc., they believed God would find them acceptable. It became something they aspired to achieve outwardly, whereas God wanted a soft heart towards Him as their Father.

Jesus had to become a man, leaving behind all the heavenly trappings, magnificence and grandeur, in order to live as a man, the life God required of mankind (which mankind was unable to live). By doing so, Jesus would achieve the standard God had put in place, and as a man, He would fulfil the law, which would win back the authority over the earth.

So, at the right moment, God sent Jesus to become a man, to live the life we cannot live because we have fallen from grace (God's standard), and He was to die in our place.

HOW DID JESUS QUALIFY?

You will probably have heard that Jesus was:

a) The Son of God, and fully God, and,

b) A man, and fully man

At first glance this doesn't seem to make sense, so let's take it apart.

Jesus needed to come to earth as a man in order to fulfil God's law (given through Moses) – something no other human being could do because all mankind is born into original sin. Thus, Jesus needed to be born of a woman – Mary – making Him a human being. We know from scripture that He was to be born of a virgin.

> [23] *"The virgin will conceive and give birth to a son, and they will call him Immanuel (which means "God with us")." (Matthew 1:23)*

At this time Mary was betrothed to Joseph, but the marriage had yet to be consummated.   However, in order not to be born into original sin, Jesus couldn't have Joseph (Mary's husband) as his father, so instead He was conceived by the Holy Spirit, giving Him a godly nature and not a human nature.

This is why He laid aside every godly attribute, leaving heaven for a lowly life on earth. He was born as a human being, lived the life of a Jew in a back-water town, learning the scriptures and walking with His Heavenly Father as He grew up, and matured into adulthood.

> [40] *And the child grew and became strong; he was filled with wisdom, and the grace of God was on him. (Luke 2:40)*

He was fully man – being born in the natural way, but He was also fully God – being conceived by the Holy Spirit. This was necessary as, if Joseph (Mary's husband) had been his father, Jesus would have inherited a carnal nature from Adam (original sin), and would not have been qualified for the task of taking back dominion over the earth.   So, He had to have God as His Father, which gave Him a godly nature. Jesus was the only member of mankind born in this way and therefore able to achieve this.

Whenever people are born-again, it is accomplished with the help of the Holy Spirit.   It is the Holy Spirit who draws us to Jesus and shows us our need of Christ as Saviour and Messiah.   So, every born-again person is regenerated – brought back into relationship with God – through the work of God's Spirit, and this enables God to live in each of us.

> [9]...if anyone does not have the Spirit of. Christ,
> they do not belong to Christ.   (Romans 8:9)

This is the starting place for our relationship with God. Further steps will be outlined later in this book.

GOD'S NATURE

Many of us may have already made a decision as to what we feel God is like. If we have read or heard some of the accounts recorded in the Old Testament, we may have seen that God issues justice and punishments at times. But this is not a complete picture of our Heavenly Father. To get the whole picture we need to know what the Bible says – both Old and New Testaments – as this is what God has given us by which to really get to know Him.

After the fall into sin in the Garden, God sent Adam and Eve out, but He did not turn His back on them, He maintained relationship with them and their descendants, although this denied the intimacy and fellowship that had been enjoyed in the Garden.

As time passed, mankind became more and more evil, and God needed to do something to stop this, and He gave the law to the Jews through Moses, and in Exodus chapter 24 the people agreed to obey it.

> [3]When Moses went and told the people all the LORD's words and laws, they responded with one voice, "Everything the LORD has said we will do." [4]Moses then wrote down everything the LORD had said. (Exodus 24:3-4)

> [7]Then he took the Book of the Covenant and read it to the people. They responded, "We will do everything the LORD has said; we will obey." (Exodus 24:7)

God gave the law to show the people what His standards are, and meant it to demonstrate they could never attain that perfect standard as they were imperfect, due to the fall. The problem was the Jews tried to fulfil the law in their own strength; that is in their own self-righteousness. They believed they could do it, without turning to God for help.

Up to this time, although people were becoming more and more sinful, God had not been keeping accounts of the people's sin.

> [13] *To be sure, sin was in the world before the law was given, but sin is not charged against anyone's account where there is no law.   (Romans 5:13)*

God did not hold their sin against them prior to the law being given.   But now the law was given, and accepted, the people would become accountable for what they did or did not do.

Because the law was in place; because the people had agreed to obey the law; and because God, although loving and merciful, is also just, He had to follow through when the people went astray.

To get a complete picture of our Heavenly Father, we need to look into the New Testament, as well as the Old.

Jesus, God's son, became a servant.   He ministered to the people; He healed them; He even washed their feet.   He came as the Servant-King.   So, does what we see in the Old Testament line up with the New Testament and actually represent who God is?

Jesus existed before the world, the universe and everything was brought into being, and the Bible describes Him thus:

> [8] *Jesus Christ is the same yesterday and today and forever.   (Hebrews 13:8)*

We also know that when Jesus was on this earth He told His disciples:

> [30] *"I and the Father are one."   (John 10:30)*

The Bible also tells us:

> [3]*The Son is the radiance of God's glory and the exact representation of his being, sustaining all things by his powerful word.   (Hebrews 1:3)*

The Message Bible translation says it like this:

> [3]*This Son perfectly mirrors God, and is stamped with God's nature. He holds everything together by what he says—powerful words!*
> *(Hebrews 1:3) (MSG)*

On one occasion when the disciples were speaking with Jesus, He said:

> [9]*"Don't you know me, Philip, even after I have been among you such a long time? Anyone who has seen me has seen the Father."   (John 14:9)*

We know that Jesus was loving and kind, and came to serve mankind as the Servant-King, teaching them God's ways and performing miracles among them. Here He is telling them that, just as they have seen Him and learnt His ways, He is just like the Father in heaven. He also taught them that He did nothing without being directed by God, so that everything He did was what His Heavenly Father wanted and approved of.

Father God may look as if He is double-minded in the Old Testament – changing His nature whenever He feels like it – but this is not true. He never changes, and His nature has always been the same. He has always wanted a family. He has always had a great love for His children. But – He is a just God, and must act justly. He must do what is right or He wouldn't be a just God. This doesn't take away from the fact that He loves people and always wants the best for them.

If you are a parent, or even if you are not, you will know that children need discipline. Parental guidance is often *tough love*. You do it to help them know the correct way to act, especially if what they do wrong will bring outcomes they do not want. For instance, we teach them not to touch the fire because they will get burnt. You might tell them that going against what you say will mean their actions will cause your reactions; for example, if they do not come home by a specific time, they will forfeit the privilege of going out for a while. You will know that having placed a boundary on your children, you need to follow through with whatever penalty you have set, so as to cause them to respect you and learn.

So it is with God. He had set out the law and they had agreed to follow it. He warned His children in the Old Testament and, as a just Father, He had to follow through when they crossed the boundaries He had put in place.

You will know that setting boundaries is a way to teach children the difference between good and bad, and also it will keep them safe. I hope you will agree that we do our children no favours if we set these boundaries and then allow them to do as they please with no consequences.

God had set boundaries for His children, and as a good Father, there were times when He also needed to follow through.

The judgements He gave are often the things we remember about Him from the Old Testament, but when we look at Him through the lens of the New Testament, we see another side of Him.

> [8]Whoever does not love does not know God, because God is love. (1 John 4:8)

This is God's real nature. He IS love. He doesn't just love; or give love; He IS love. If you could turn Him around, whichever way you saw Him, you would see He is love.

God's kind of love is different from what most of us humans experience. His kind of love is always doing the right thing. His kind of love is always forgiving and wanting the best for the person that is loved.

> [4]Love is patient, love is kind. It does not envy, it does not boast, it is not proud. [5]It does not dishonour others, it is not self-seeking, it is not easily angered, it keeps no record of wrongs. [6]Love does not delight in evil but rejoices with the truth. [7]It always protects, always trusts, always hopes, always perseveres. [8]Love never fails.
> (1 Corinthians 13:4-8)

This is who your Heavenly Father really is. This is how He wants to look after you, if you will allow Him to do so.

In a nutshell:

- o The Old Testament shows us how much **God hates sin**; because it corrupts and ruins lives and takes us away from Him.

- o The New Testament shows us how much **God loves us** and wants to rescue us from the ravages of sin, which He did by sending His most precious gift – Jesus – to deal with the sin problem.

When you look at Jesus in the New Testament, remember that He is the express image of His Father (and our Father) in heaven.

Chapter 3

What's In It For Us?

We have seen what happened in the Garden of Eden, and we have seen how God had a plan already in place to put things right, but where do we stand now, and how do we benefit from this?

In this chapter we will look at some of what was achieved for us by Jesus dying on the cross.

FORGIVENESS

It was sin that had destroyed our intimacy with God in the beginning. Now that Jesus had fulfilled the law and suffered and died in our place, the way was open for this relationship to be restored. His blood was shed on the cross for our sin, and by it we are redeemed. What does redemption actually mean?

The noun *redemption* means the process of being redeemed, and to be redeemed is to be bought back by the original owner – like when we surrender something to a pawn broker, and if we want it back a price has to be paid.

As a three-part being – spirit, soul and body – we have learnt that our spirit, once dead and separated from God, can be made fully alive again to God through Jesus. This takes place the instant a person is born-again.

Our soul is where our personality resides, along with our emotions and thinking. This part of us remains the same after being born-again. However, we are told in the Bible to renew our minds to the Word of God.

> *[2]Do not conform to the pattern of this world, but be transformed by the renewing of your mind. Then you will be able to test and approve what God's will is—his good, pleasing and perfect will. (Romans 12:2)*

This is something we need to do for ourselves. God will not do it for us! He gave us free will, and He desires that we choose to pursue Him. Renewing our minds brings about change in our soul. This verse explains that when we choose to renew our minds, we will less and less think like our old selves (our nature received from Adam), and come into line with how God thinks, and in so doing we will discover God's will for our lives. God has a plan and purpose for each one of us, and it is in our journey with Him that we discover what our particular plan and purpose is. We renew our minds by reading God's Word and becoming familiar with it.

> [11] *"For I know the plans I have for you," declares the LORD, "plans to prosper you and not to harm you, plans to give you hope and a future."*
> *(Jeremiah 29:11)*

Our bodies also do not change. They will remain the same:

> [16] *Therefore we do not lose heart. Though outwardly we are wasting away, yet inwardly we are being renewed day by day. (2 Corinthians 4:16)*

but we will change inside (in our souls) as we walk with God and discover His Word.

> [1] *We are convinced that even if these bodies we live in are folded up at death like tents, we will still have a God-built home that no human hands have built, which will last forever in the heavenly realm.*
> *(2 Corinthians 5:1) (TPT)*

And here is God's promise of a new, supernatural body to come, for those who belong to Him.

So we see, that part of our redemption is immediate and enduring (our spirits are changed and made alive); whilst our souls are not changed but will change along the way, as we walk with God and focus on His Word; and our bodies, although changing with the aging process, will be gloriously changed into an everlasting body after we have left this earth.

JUSTIFICATION

To justify something is an act of making something right. You can be justified in holding a certain view if it is proved correct, and we need to be justified before God – that is, made right with God.

We looked at the fact that everyone falls short of God's standard:

> *[3]...for all have sinned and fall short of the glory of God, (Romans 3:23)*

and we know that God had a plan of redemption for mankind, so justification becomes part of the benefit package we receive on being born-again. To put it simply – it is peace with God. How can this be possible because we know we have all sinned and fallen short?

When Jesus came to earth – fully man and fully God – He was able to live the life that we couldn't live, keeping God's high standard and still be without sin. In so doing, Jesus fulfilled God's law (the ten commandments) and became the one person on the planet for all time, who could take back the authority over the earth that Adam had given away. God was looking for a man to accomplish this, and He found him in Jesus. Now the earth belongs to Jesus the man. In achieving this, Jesus dealt with the sin problem once for all time.

Being born-again means that the blood Jesus shed on the cross is used for our benefit by cleansing us from sin. Even before the cross, God was merciful, kind and forgiving.

> *[18]"Come now, let us settle the matter," says the LORD. "Though your sins are like scarlet, they shall be as white as snow; though they are red as crimson, they shall be like wool." (Isaiah 1:18)*

Even in the Old Testament, God was showing through this verse in Isaiah that He would forgive the people's sin.

> *²²In fact, the law requires that nearly everything be cleansed with blood, and without the shedding of blood there is no forgiveness. (Hebrews 9:22)*

Until Jesus came, sin was atoned for by animal sacrifice, because without the shedding of blood there is no forgiveness for sin. When Jesus was crucified, He became the final sacrifice for sin, and took all sin in His body on the cross. Because He was the perfect lamb, there is now no longer a need for animal sacrifice.

> *²⁹The next day John saw Jesus coming toward him and said, "Look, the Lamb of God, who takes away the sin of the world!" (John 1:29)*

John the Baptist was the forerunner of Jesus, declaring His coming, and who He was – the perfect sacrifice. Jesus' perfect sacrifice has allowed us to be justified before God.

St Paul tells us:

> *¹Therefore, since we have been justified through faith, we have peace with God through our Lord Jesus Christ, ²through whom we have gained access by faith into this grace in which we now stand. (Romans 5:1-2)*

RIGHTEOUSNESS

Here's another long word, usually attributed to Jesus, and the Bible refers to it as a garment.

> *¹⁰I delight greatly in the LORD; my soul rejoices in my God. For he has clothed me with garments of*

> *salvation and arrayed me in a robe of his*
> *righteousness, as a bridegroom adorns his head*
> *like a priest, and as a bride adorns herself with her*
> *jewels. (Isaiah 61:10)*

So the robe of righteousness is something we wear. We can only do this once we have been born-again and received salvation, and it is something we receive from God. Although it is invisible to us, the spiritual realm sees it on us and knows to whom we belong! Being born-again transfers us from the kingdom of darkness into the kingdom of God's glorious light.

> *¹³For he has rescued us from the dominion of*
> *darkness and brought us into the kingdom of the*
> *Son he loves. (Colossians 1:13)*

Before we come to know Jesus personally (being born-again) we operate in our own righteousness which God looks on as filthy rags, stained by sin.

> *⁶All of us have become like one who is unclean,*
> *and all our righteous acts are like filthy rags; we all*
> *shrivel up like a leaf, and like the wind our sins*
> *sweep us away. (Isaiah 64:6)*

Although we do not deserve anything from God, once we are born-again, He has chosen to array us in His robe of righteousness. What good father (and He is the best) would not want his children looking splendid.

RECONCILIATION

The heart of the Father is one of reconciliation. He wanted to put things right between mankind and Himself, and this

He did through Jesus, and has made everything possible to this end. It is now up to mankind to make the right choice. He will never force us into relationship with Him, but His heart is always for us.

By being born-again we enter this relationship. Our citizenship is registered in heaven, and eternal life begins here and now on earth. Our relationship with Him changes us. We begin to think differently; we stop being fearful about things like the future; we know peace in our hearts, which deepens over time.

> [16]*For God so loved the world that he gave his one and only Son, that whoever believes in him shall not perish but have eternal life.   (John 3:16)*

> [24]*"Very truly I tell you, whoever hears my word and believes him who sent me has eternal life and will not be judged but has crossed over from death to life."   (John 5:24)*

> [11]*And this is the testimony: God has given us eternal life, and this life is in his Son.   (1 John 5:11)*

> [3]*Now this is eternal life: that they know you, the only true God, and Jesus Christ, whom you have sent.   (John 17:3)*

These verses speak of eternal life being received here on earth.   1 John 5:11 confirms that we find eternal life through Jesus, and the final verse – John 17:3 – tells us that knowing the Father through Jesus *is* eternal life.

Eternal life is intimacy with God – our earthly picture to demonstrate this being marriage. Imagine the very best marriage you can, and you can begin to get a flavour of my meaning. We experience it now; we don't wait until we get to heaven; we can know the joy, the love, the closeness, in fact everything that God has to offer can be experienced right now.

ADOPTION

We have already looked at how God wanted a family and put Adam into the Garden of Eden with purposes – one of which was to multiply and fill the earth. God had made Adam in His own likeness and image and wanted Adam to produce offspring in the same likeness and image, thus creating a huge family. God has a Father's heart.

We have also learnt what went wrong and how mankind was separated from God by the sin of disobedience, and we have looked at how Jesus came to earth with the express intention of taking back what Adam had given away.

We then went on to see that if we choose to be born-again, we are adopted into God's family and become part of his Kingdom. Jesus is the gateway through which we can enter into God's family.

> *7Therefore Jesus said again, "Very truly I tell you, I am the gate for the sheep. (John 10:7)*

> *9I am the gate; whoever enters through me will be saved. (John 10:9)*

Here again we remind ourselves of Ephesians 1.

> *4For he chose us in him before the creation of the world to be holy and blameless in his sight. In love 5he predestined us for adoption to sonship*

*through Jesus Christ, in accordance with his
pleasure and will. (Ephesians 1:4-5)*

Now when you are a member of a family there is nothing
you can do to change that. In John 8:35 we can see that
being a family member is a forever thing.

> *[8]Now a slave has no permanent place in the family,
> but a son belongs to it forever. (John 8:35)*

Of course, we can decide to have nothing to do with our
relatives, but it doesn't change the fact that we are related
to them.

Families have their own idiosyncrasies and ways of doing
things. Some are musical or sporty or academic – the list
could go on. Traits tend to run in families.

When we are born-again and therefore adopted into God's
family, we re-gain God's nature. Remember when Adam
lost his godly nature because he chose to follow what
Satan said through the serpent? Adoption brings us back
into fellowship with God and our nature is now a godly one;
we become part of the family of God, adopted as a son,
and become a co-heir with Jesus in all God has.

> *[17]Now if we are children, then we are heirs—heirs
> of God and co-heirs with Christ, if indeed we share
> in his sufferings in order that we may also share in
> his glory. (Romans 8:17)*

This verse is not referring to worldly wealth and success, it
refers to spiritual matters. The Christian life is not always a
bed of roses, but fulfils and satisfies as nothing else can.
We will still go through uncomfortable situations, but now
God will be there with us in whatever we go through.

THE LAW FULFILLED!

God gave the law through Moses because mankind was becoming more and more evil. The people followed it as best they could, but could never reach God's high standard, thereby missing the mark. This is why Jesus came. He *could* reach the standard. He was the only one who could fulfil the law of God.

> [17] *"Do not think that I have come to abolish the Law or the Prophets; I have not come to abolish them but to fulfill them. (Matthew 5:17)*

Without Jesus we would have no hope. But – Jesus came and fulfilled the law on our behalf. He took our place; fulfilled everything the Father required; died in our place; went to hell in our place; and rose from the dead.

Now we have a new beginning.

With the law fulfilled, does this mean we can do what we like? Looking around the world we can sometimes think so, and indeed God will not overrule our free will. Being born-again with a godly nature gives us the opportunity to change as we walk with Him.

But for us who are born-again, Jesus has dealt with the law – and replaced it with something new.

> [34] *"A new command I give you: Love one another. As I have loved you, so you must love one another." (John 13:34)*

Instead of *thou shalt not* (the law), we are instructed to love. The type of love here is total – our whole being needs to be involved. How is it possible? Well, once we are born-again, we have the Holy Spirit in us and, just as He helped

Jesus to do all He did while on earth, so the Spirit will help us also.

This new commandment, when carried out properly, encompasses all the *thou shalt nots* of the law. How does it do that? When we really love God (being born-again with a new nature), we no longer desire to covet and hate and abuse. Need help to do this? Just ask your Heavenly Father.

EVER PRESENT HELP

Our born-again spirit – being made new and alive – is now a clean, beautiful place, and God Himself has come to reside there. He now lives in us and has promised never to leave us or forsake us.

> *[5]Keep your lives free from the love of money and be content with what you have, because God has said, "Never will I leave you, never will I forsake you". (Hebrews 13:5)*

I don't know what your background is, or what you have been through in life, but whether it was a good experience or not, no matter what we have undergone, God lives inside those who are born-again and has promised to stay with them forever. You need never again be alone. Everywhere you go, He will be with you. Everything you go through, He will go through it with you. He is your ever-present help in time of trouble.

> *[1]God is our refuge and strength, an ever-present help in trouble. (Psalm 46:1)*

God always keeps His promises. He is faithful, trustworthy and true, and you can rely on Him. What He says in His

Word, He means; and what He means, He tells us in His Word. He will lead and guide you if you will allow Him to do so. Keep your heart soft and humble before Him.

IT IS FINISHED

These very words are mentioned in the Bible, but what are they referring to, and how should they be applied?

> *[30]When he had received the drink, Jesus said, "It is finished". With that, he bowed his head and gave up his spirit. (John 19:30)*

Here is Jesus on the cross. He was given vinegar to drink immediately before he spoke these words, and we see that it is Jesus who brought His own life to an end by releasing His spirit. Jesus was willing to go through this in order to secure our redemption (buying us back). He was willing to stay alive, enduring the suffering on the cross, until the moment everything had been fulfilled and carried out to the Father's specification. Then, He gave up His spirit.

So, you might ask, what is it that is finished?

Jesus came to fulfil the law, which mankind could not do – this He fulfilled to the letter; absolutely everything the Father required was carried out by the Son in order to purchase (buy back) people for God. There was a price to be paid, and Jesus paid that price in full on the cross.

> *[9]And they sang a new song, saying: "You are worthy to take the scroll and to open its seals, because you were slain, and with your blood you purchased for God persons from every tribe and language and people and nation. (Revelation 5:9)*

But the words *it is finished* mean more than that. By fulfilling the law; doing everything the Father required; dying in our place; the way was now open to heaven through Jesus.

There had been in the Temple in Jerusalem, a huge, heavy curtain, believed to be 10cms (4") thick, over 9m (30 feet) high, which separated the Holy Place (where the priests ministered to God), from the Most Holy Place (where the Ark of the Covenant was kept, and where God's presence resided). It was only the High Priest who could enter the Most Holy Place, and then only once a year. He needed to consecrate himself for this, as to not do so would cause him to die in God's presence as he entered. At the moment of Jesus' death, the curtain was torn in two, from top to bottom – notice it was not from bottom to top. It was so thick and heavy it could not have been torn by a man. However, the miracle here is that God Himself tore the curtain from the top all the way down. Why? He did it in order to show that the way to God, which had been damaged and changed by sin, was now open to all. It was no longer just for the High Priest, but for everyone who would response to God's call in their life.

Due to Jesus' perfect life as a man; by His taking our place on the cross; by His going to hell instead of us, and rising from the dead; He had finished the work (the plan and purpose) the Father had assigned for Him on earth. He completed everything necessary for our reconciliation to the Father. There is now NOTHING further that needs to be done – all we have to do is believe it and receive it. We do this by faith – which is simply to choose to trust our Heavenly Father and His Word. We cannot add to it, it is already perfect. We cannot earn it or merit it, for we are all fallen people. We can only receive it with thanks. It is a complete work – it is finished!

FREE, GRATIS & FOR NOTHING

The title of this segment uses three statements all meaning the same thing. If something is *free*, you don't pay for it. The word *gratis* means without charge or payment; something given with favour. Finally, *for nothing* speaks for itself.

What Jesus did at the cross in simple words is – He was punished in our place, which means we can go free if we receive Him.   We are the guilty ones who deserved punishment, but the punishment for sin is death!

> [23]*For the wages of sin is death,   (Romans 6:23)*

We now know that death in the Bible refers to separation from God (which is eternal darkness after we die), but, this verse goes on to say:

> [23]*...but the gift of God is eternal life in Christ Jesus our Lord.   (Romans 6:23)*

Hallelujah, there is now a way out of our predicament, and it costs us nothing. However, it cost Jesus everything. But, he loves us so much that He considered us worth dying for.

PART 2

Chapter 4

Where Do We Go From Here?

So what happens next? Becoming a Christian isn't a final goal – it is only the first step in your walk with the living God. Real life starts here. Some Christians will, at this point, get comfortable and not move forward in any way, but God has a plan and a purpose for every person which He wants us to pursue. Notice it is for us to pursue! So our next step is to find out what that plan and purpose is.

This purpose will be different for each of us. We are each uniquely made, and each have a unique plan awaiting us.

Adam found out his purpose by spending time with God. They talked together in the Garden and God explained what Adam's task was.

We too can find out our purpose by spending time talking with God (in prayer) – in speaking to Him and listening to His answer. However, God also speaks through His Word and a good starting place is in reading the Bible, which will give understanding of how His Kingdom works and how we fit into it.

This is especially true in the New Testament of the Bible, which gives the account of Jesus' life on earth and how the disciples were called, grew in understanding, became born-again, and were sent out to spread the good news of the Kingdom of God. The Old Testament acts to confirm and reinforce what we see in the New Testament.

THE WORD

Most of us know a bit about what's in the Bible. Maybe we learnt a little at school or Sunday School. Maybe we have attended church for a while and we hear some verses read out on a Sunday during the service. Most people don't read the Bible on a regular basis or, if they do, it is only a few verses during their devotional time (a short quiet time spent with God), as they begin their day. We need to get into it with some real study in order to get a grasp on what it says.

The Psalmist describes the Word of God like this:

> [105]*Your words are a flashlight to light the path ahead of me and keep me from stumbling.*
> *(Psalm 119:105) (TLB)*

The Bible describes itself in these terms:

> [12]*For the word of God is alive and active. Sharper than any double-edged sword, it penetrates even to dividing soul and spirit, joints and marrow; it judges the thoughts and attitudes of the heart.*
> *(Hebrews 4:12)*

The Word of God is different from other writing. The Bible is different from every other book ever written. How so? It is because its words are alive and active. They are supernatural words, coming from a supernatural God. They accomplish things. As we read them, they will speak to us and give us understanding and wisdom. They will guide us in how to navigate different situations. This verse describes how God's Word can divide our soul (our thinking part that is in the process of change) from our spirit (which has been redeemed and made whole with God).

It not only gives us this spiritual help and understanding, but can deal with our bodies and its needs (joints and marrow), while at the same time show us if our heart attitudes are right or wrong.

God's Word is a measuring rod or plumb line by which we can change and bring our lives into line with Him.

> *17Sanctify them by the truth; your word is truth.*
> *(John 17:17)*

John 17:17 is part of a prayer of Jesus to His Father. He is praying about His disciples just prior to His crucifixion, asking that they be sanctified by God's Word. These words were not only for His disciples, but also for us who have come after. As we read and ponder the Word, we will change in our soulish realm, which will sanctify us.

To be sanctified is to be set apart for God and His purposes as we change. This should be our intention as we follow Him.

> *4Then he taught me, and he said to me, "Take hold of my words with all your heart; keep my commands, and you will live. 5Get wisdom, get understanding; do not forget my words or turn away from them." (Proverbs 4:4-5)*

God's Word will teach you and bring you into a degree of understanding you did not previously have, which will result in wisdom.

> *89Your word, LORD, is eternal; it stands firm in the heavens. (Psalm 119:89)*

Another version of this Psalm says it like this:

> *89Forever, O Lord, Your word is settled in heaven. (Psalm 119:89) (NKJV)*

So we see that the Word of God is unchangeable. God always says what He means, and means what He says! Another reason we can rely on God's Word is found in Isaiah:

> [11]...so is my word that goes out from my mouth: It will not return to me empty, but will accomplish what I desire and achieve the purpose for which I sent it. (Isaiah 55:11)

The Word of God is powerful; it always does the job it is assigned to do; it never changes. We human beings often change our minds – sometimes because we are fickle, sometimes because we haven't thought a thing through properly and now see it from a different angle – but whatever the reason, changing our minds is something we do. However, God is different.

> [19]God is not human, that he should lie, not a human being, that he should change his mind. Does he speak and then not act? Does he promise and not fulfil? (Numbers 23:19)

God's Word has been spoken (the Bible) and settled in heaven for all time. Furthermore, God doesn't alter or vary what He has said. In fact, we have here an example from each of the Old and New Testaments confirming that whatever happens, the Word of God will never pass away.

> [8]"The grass withers and the flowers fall, but the word of our God endures forever." (Isaiah 40:8)

> [25]"...but the word of the Lord endures forever." And this is the word that was preached to you. (1 Peter 1:25)

The Bible was written over many years by a number of different people. However, Bible scholars agree there is a flow and agreement throughout the Bible confirming that the Holy Spirit is indeed the author.

> *[16]All Scripture is God-breathed and is useful for teaching, rebuking, correcting and training in righteousness. (2 Timothy 3:16)*

The Holy Spirit has linked everything together, and has inspired and influenced each writer, which brings the Bible together as a whole. Some people consider there are discrepancies in God's Word, but a thorough study of the Word (Old and New Testaments) will bring clarity and unity of understanding.

Because the Bible is so reliable it is really helpful if we can memorise verses here and there. If you are faithful in reading your Bible, you will find that this will happen automatically.   One of the roles of the Holy Spirit is to bring back to our remembrance truths we have discovered, and He can do it – after all, He is the author!

> *[26]But the Advocate, the Holy Spirit, whom the Father will send in my name, will teach you all things and will remind you of everything I have said to you. (John 14:26)*

When I was a young Christian, I came across this verse and decided that if the Holy Spirit was going to function in my life in this way, I needed to have read the Bible all the way through. How could He remind me of things if I hadn't read them! So I set about reading God's Word. Since then, I have done this many times and, in fact, each time I reach the end, I start again.

My first attempt took quite a long time. I had no idea of the best way of doing this and started at Genesis and worked through to Revelation. However, there are better ways. You can find Bible reading plans on the internet. There are quite a few to choose from, so there will be one to suit your style of reading and learning. I also change the version from which I am reading, as it can be helpful in getting more of an overview of what God is saying.

Don't just read it like a newspaper – take small bites and chew them thoroughly, asking God to give you understanding of the content – that way you will gain so much more from your reading, and you will grow and mature as a Christian.

When we are born-again we become new creations in Christ. To find out what that means, we need to look at what the Bible says. The Bible speaks a lot about us, and when we discover something it says about us, we will benefit and change if we agree with it, no matter what we previously thought. In addition, when we read what it tells us to do, it is wisdom for us to do the things God says – He only wants the best for us, and it will benefit us.

It is a fact that we have never seen our own face. If we need to check whether our face is clean or our hair is tidy, we look into a mirror. It shows us what we need to know, and we take note of it, and make adjustments according to what we see. Similarly, as we look into the Bible, we see things about ourselves that need to be adjusted or changed.

The book of James tells us this:

> [23]Anyone who listens to the word but does not do what it says is like someone who looks at his face in a mirror [24]and, after looking at himself, goes away and immediately forgets what he looks like.[25]But whoever looks intently into the perfect law that gives freedom, and continues in it—not forgetting what they have heard, but doing it— they will be blessed in what they do.
> (James 1:23-25)

Verse 25 speaks of the *perfect law*. This is not the law of Moses under the Old Covenant – that law has been fulfilled by Jesus Christ. It refers to the New Covenant, brought in by the death and resurrection of our Lord. We need to pay attention to, and do, what we read and hear.

So let's make the main thing, the main thing – let's read our Bibles.

God always wants the best for us. He never will harm us. If He calls for us to do something, it is always for our good, and He equips us for any task.

> [31]If God is for us, who can be against us?
> (Romans 8:31)

ME, THE CENTRE OF MY UNIVERSE!

We know that God is three persons in one – Father, Son and Holy Spirit – and we also know we are made in His likeness – spirit, soul and body.

> [23]*May God himself, the God of peace, sanctify you through and through. May your whole spirit, soul and body be kept blameless at the coming of our Lord Jesus Christ. (1 Thessalonians 5:23)*

Although it is very clear from the above scripture that we are three-part beings, not all Christians understand how these three, function together. There are some who think that our spirit and our soul are basically the same, so let's look into this a little further.

Our body is the obvious part – it's a part of us that we can see and feel. Our soul is less so, but also obvious – it's the part of us where our emotions, personality and thinking are. These two parts are in touch with one another. If I am cold, my body will let me know. If I am happy, my soul will express it. I can instantly know how I am feeling because I am in touch with both these parts of me, and they interact with one another. We are aware of these two parts of ourselves. However, our spirits are a little different.

Before we are born-again, our spirit rules. It is our centre – and it tells us what it wants to do. It is – I want; I'm going to have; I'm going to do! Remember it is made in the likeness of Adam's fallen nature and this is what he and Eve in the Garden did – they acted independently of Father God and *did their own thing!*

It is a case of majority rules – so long as two out of three parts of my being agree to wanting a thing, then the third part goes along with it. It is usually our spirit and soul wanting to do something and our body just tags along for the ride. However, once we are born-again, things change.

Now, my spirit is renewed to God. Now, my spirit is made perfect by the Holy Spirit. Now, it agrees with God in all things. The challenge is, getting the information held there, from our new born-again spirit, into our thinking part – our souls.

Our spirit has now been renewed by God and is perfect. This part of us is already redeemed. Remember, we are not in the process of change in our spirit, we are a new creation, immediately transformed when we are born-again.

Our spirit is now where God resides – it is no longer where I rule. We need to get in touch with our spirit. We do this through getting to know what God's Word says. As we grow in the knowledge of the scriptures (Bible), our soul begins to agree with God's Word and it changes us. For example, if my renewed spirit (now made in the image of God) believes in healing of the body (which it does), and my soul reads in the Word that God heals today, and if I can move in faith, then my body must change in line with the Word of God and be healed.

In this way we draw out of our spirits the wisdom and truth that allow us to enjoy our lives now. This is part of the eternal life package we receive at the moment of the new birth.

Chapter 5

Baptisms

You are probably aware of the term baptism. This book is looking at, among other things, three different baptisms spoken of in the Bible. The first we covered in Part 1, as being born-again into the Kingdom of God is actually a baptism performed by the Holy Spirit.   It is He who draws people who are searching for truth, into God's family.   At the moment of being born-again we are baptised into the Body of Christ.   We become part of His Body.   This is confirmed in 1 Corinthians 12:

> *12Just as a body, though one, has many parts, but all its many parts form one body, so it is with Christ. 13For we were all baptized by one Spirit so as to*

form one body—whether Jews or Gentiles, slave or free—and we were all given the one Spirit to drink. ¹⁴Even so the body is not made up of one part but of many. (1 Corinthians 12:12-14)

²⁷Now you are the body of Christ, and each one of you is a part of it. (1 Corinthians 12:27)

At that moment we are all given purpose and gifts to use for God, and from this time on we need to learn and grow, just as a baby needs to learn and grow, as we discover what our purpose and gifts are.

There are two further baptisms we will look at, the first being baptism in water.

BAPTISM IN WATER

Baptism in water is different from a Christening, which is a sprinkling (usually, but not always, of babies). A Christening of babies is sometimes known as a naming ceremony and can involve adults making promises on behalf of the child.

Water baptism is where a person has been born-again, and is completely immersed in water as a sign of an old life having died and is being buried, and a new life rising up out of the water. It's a bit like a funeral service and needs only to be carried out once.

> *⁴We were therefore buried with him through baptism into death in order that, just as Christ was raised from the dead through the glory of the*

> *Father, we too may live a new life.   (Romans 6:4)*

> *[12]...having been buried with him in baptism, in which you were also raised with him through your faith in the working of God, who raised him from the dead.   (Colossians 2:12)*

Water baptism was not a new thing in Bible times. There were ceremonial washings required of the Jews, and John the Baptist baptised people for repentance – that is, he would baptise by immersion in water those who wished to repent of their sin, saying sorry to God for what they had done. This was just prior to Jesus' ministry and was not to do with being born-again.

> *[4]And so John the Baptist appeared in the wilderness, preaching a baptism of repentance for the forgiveness of sins. (Mark 1:4)*

The word *repent* does not mean groveling in the dirt before God, but actually means:

- o recognising your actions in life have been against what God wants, and saying sorry;

- o changing your thinking;

- o making a U-turn from the way you lead your life.

To repent means a complete change, which being born-again, is. It is the Holy Spirit who highlights our sinful nature, when we just know deep within ourselves our need for God's forgiveness, and the Spirit will draw us to Jesus, who is the gateway to the Kingdom of Heaven.

Baptism in water should follow being born-again, and is not really an option but a command. Why should it be so? Well, being born-again is entry level into the Kingdom of God and water baptism completes the process. It is an act of separation from the old life and into the new. We are in the world and saved by faith in what Jesus has done, and baptism separates us from the past. Jesus spoke the following words.

> *[15]He said to them, "Go into all the world and preach the gospel to all creation. [16]Whoever believes and is baptized will be saved, but whoever does not believe will be condemned."* (Mark 16:15-16)

Christians sometimes decide not to take this step of water baptism, often because they feel it can be embarrassing, but it is a step of obedience and a marvelous experience. When I was invited to be baptised in water, I really didn't want to do it. I was a bit of a wallflower who didn't like the limelight, but I decided to be obedient, and afterwards I felt nine feet tall. I would, therefore, urge all of you to seriously consider this step, especially as it completes your entry into God's Kingdom, separating you from your old life.

We can see from the following scripture that we are all called upon to be born-again followed by baptism in water, but it doesn't stop there.

^{38}Peter replied, "Repent and be baptized, every one of you, in the name of Jesus Christ for the forgiveness of your sins. And you will receive the gift of the Holy Spirit." (Acts 2:38)

What is this gift referred to here? It is the baptism of the Holy Spirit, which we will look at next.

BAPTISM OF THE HOLY SPIRIT

Our third baptism is the baptism of the Holy Spirit – sometimes called *being filled with the Holy Spirit* – and can only happen after we are born-again.

Until the time of Jesus' crucifixion, resurrection and return to heaven, the Holy Spirit came to people only as and when He had a special job for them to do. He would come upon people (those specifically needed for that task), but would depart once the job was done. The Holy Spirit was in the earth actively helping, leading and guiding, and would only come upon people for a purpose. There are no exceptions to this.

John the Baptist was called upon to prepare the way for Jesus' coming, when Jesus would bring to a conclusion the Old Covenant (under Moses), and usher in the New Covenant in Himself as Messiah. This, John accomplished with help from the Holy Spirit who came upon him for this task. John was not born-again as his life, ministry and death took place prior to the crucifixion, and he is listed as the last prophet of the Old Covenant. Although John was blessed with the Holy Spirit in order to carry out his ministry prior to Messiah Jesus being revealed, he did not receive the in-filling of the Spirit as described in the book of The Acts of the Apostles. The baptism of John did not replace the water baptism that believers are to undergo; he was highlighting the people's need for forgiveness as he proclaimed the coming of the Messiah, who would deal with the sin of the world.

The baptism of the Holy Spirit is confused by some, that being born-again automatically means you are filled with Him. Scripture clearly tells us this is not so. Although these two events can take place almost simultaneously, they are separate experiences, and we have good examples of this in scripture. Let's take a look at what the book of John says.

> *[19]On the evening of that first day of the week, when the disciples were together, with the doors locked for fear of the Jewish leaders, Jesus came and stood among them and said, "Peace be with you!" [20]After he said this, he showed them his hands and side. The disciples were overjoyed when they saw the Lord.*
>
> *[21]Again Jesus said, "Peace be with you! As the Father has sent me, I am sending you." [22]And with that he breathed on them and said, "Receive the Holy Spirit." (John 20: 19-22)*

This event took place on the evening of the day that Jesus was resurrected from the dead (Easter Day). He was still a man, but He now had His resurrection body, and although the doors were locked because the disciples were frightened, Jesus was able to just appear in the room as His new body was supernatural.

In verse 22 we see that Jesus *breathed* on them and said 'receive the Holy Spirit'. Back in the Garden of Eden in Genesis 2:7 the Bible says:

> [7]*Then the* LORD *God formed a man from the dust of the ground and breathed into his nostrils the breath of life, and the man became a living being. (Genesis 2:7)*

This is the account of when God made Adam alive with the ability to commune with Him, receiving His life and nature, by breathing into Adam's nostrils. The same word for *breath* is used in both these verses (this one and John 20:22), signifying the same meaning of bringing to life with God's life and nature.

We know that through Adam, we lost our closeness with God because our spirit died due to sin, and we also know that Jesus came to earth as a man in order to take back the authority over the earth that Adam had given away. We looked at being born-again in Part 1, and this verse – John 20:22 – records the moment of being born-again for the disciples present at that gathering, when their spirits became alive to God and they received a new nature. This is also the moment when the church came into being.

Notice that these men were fearful of the Jewish leaders. After all, they had just seen their Saviour taken from them, tried and crucified. Yes, they had now seen His risen person, but they were afraid of what the future might hold for them. When Jesus appeared, He breathed new life into them. This life was the life of God in them, and they were born-again, but they were still frightened.

Jesus remained on the earth for 40 days before ascending to heaven. Just before He left planet earth, He gave them a message.

> [8]*"...you will receive power when the Holy Spirit comes on you; and you will be my witnesses in Jerusalem, and in all Judea and Samaria, and to the ends of the earth."* [9]*After he said this, he was taken up before their very eyes, and a cloud hid him from their sight.* (Acts 1:8-9)

Earlier we looked at Jesus breathing on the disciples – their born-again moment, and the birth of the church – and here we see that there will be a further experience when the Holy Spirit will come upon each of them and fill them. After being born-again, the disciples remained fearful, locking themselves away for safety. The infilling is the presence of the Holy Spirit in power. Remember under the Old Covenant the Holy Spirit only came *upon* people to give them the power to effect particular tasks for God, and then departed. Here we see that He will come *upon* the disciples, filling them – everyone born-again can be filled with the Holy Spirit, which empowers us in living this new life in God.

Jesus told the disciples to stay in Jerusalem until they received the Holy Spirit – He knew they would need the Spirit's power. You might wonder – didn't they receive the Holy Spirit when they were born-again? Well yes, but this was not the 'coming upon, in-filling' of this baptism, it was to enable them to be born-again into the Body of Christ. When we are born-again, we receive the Spirit inside us – it is like a well of water from which we can drink. When we are filled with the Spirit, He comes upon us and fills us – He becomes likes a river within us, gushing out in power.

Another example is found in Acts chapter 8. It follows the first recorded account of Christian martyrdom, when they were scattered throughout Judea and Samaria as they sought to escape persecution, and shows the difference in the disciples now they were filled with God's power.

> *[4]Those who had been scattered preached the word wherever they went. [5]Philip went down to a city in Samaria and proclaimed the Messiah there. [6]When the crowds heard Philip and saw the signs he performed, they all paid close attention to what he said. [7]For with shrieks, impure spirits came out of many, and many who were paralyzed or lame were healed. [8]So there was great joy in that city.*
> *(Acts 8:4-8)*

Philip, one of the disciples known as Philip the Evangelist, went to Samaria where he not only preached, but followed it with demonstrations of the Kingdom by carrying out signs and wonders (miracles and acts of healing).

> *[14]When the apostles in Jerusalem heard that Samaria had accepted the word of God, they sent Peter and John to Samaria. [15]When they arrived, they prayed for the new believers there that they might receive the Holy Spirit, [16]because the Holy Spirit had not yet come on any of them; they had simply been baptized in the name of the Lord Jesus. [17]Then Peter and John placed their hands on them, and they received the Holy Spirit.*
> *(Acts 8:14-17)*

News got back to Jerusalem of the exploits done by Philip, and Peter and John went to Samaria to follow up on this work. When they arrived, they discovered that the people had indeed received Jesus as Messiah and Lord, but they had not been baptised with the Holy Spirit. This demonstrates quite clearly that being *born-again* and being *filled with the Holy Spirit* are two separate occurrences.

So you can be a born-again Christian but **not** Spirit-filled, but you cannot be filled with the Spirit of God if you are **not** a born-again Christian.

If all I have related here has not yet convinced you of this, then let us take a look at the Lord Himself.

Jesus was born as a man, and had a godly nature from His Father in heaven through being conceived supernaturally. This nature is what we also receive when we are born-again. He was without sin – very necessary as He was to fulfil the law of Moses, which required perfection – and He lived a perfect life. We hear virtually nothing of Him growing up into manhood, until He presents Himself to John the Baptist for water baptism. John was baptising in water for repentance. However, Jesus was sinless and did not need this baptism, but here He was identifying with mankind and being obedient to His Father's will. At the moment He rose up out of the water, the Holy Spirit came upon Him and filled Him. If Jesus needed the power of the baptism of the Holy Spirit when He was the perfect Son of God, how much more do we imperfect people also need the Spirit's power!

Although Jesus was pure and sinless with a godly nature His ministry did not begin until He was filled with the Spirit. The infilling of God's Holy Spirit is God's power-house. The man Jesus needed God's power of the Spirit in order to carry out His purpose on earth. Similarly, the ministry of the disciples also did not begin until they were filled with the Holy Spirit. Surely we also need this baptism in order to be able to carry out our purpose in this life. So how do we go about receiving this baptism?

We read earlier in Acts 2:38 that this baptism is a gift – and we see from scripture (both Old and New Testaments) that it is given by God. It comes from Him; we cannot just take it. It is His, and when He gives it, we can receive it.

The following passage tells us to *ask* our Heavenly Father for this gift of being filled with the Holy Spirit.

> [11]*"Which of you fathers, if your son asks for a fish, will give him a snake instead? [12]Or if he asks for an egg, will give him a scorpion? [13]If you then, though you are evil, know how to give good gifts to your children, how much more will your Father in heaven give the Holy Spirit to those who ask him!"* (Luke 11:11-13)

I believe this is not just referring to a quick, polite, formal request; it is not about asking today, and tomorrow forgetting about it; it is desiring with your heart as you bring your request before God. God only gives good gifts, and He wants you to have this one.

This baptism in the Holy Spirit can be imparted in various ways. These are the ways I have so far come across in my walk with God. We can receive it by asking, as explained above; it can be received when others pray for us, or when we have the laying on of hands for this purpose (as seen in the passage in Acts 8:14-17 above); it can come when we rise up out of the water following water baptism, which was the way Jesus received this; and, it can come because we need it and God sees our heart and just provides. This last example is my own experience, and I refer to this later in this chapter.

The following verse tells us what the purpose of this gift of God is.

> [8]*...you will receive power when the Holy Spirit comes on you; and you will be my witnesses in Jerusalem, and in all Judea and Samaria, and to the ends of the earth." (Acts 1:8)*

The Holy Spirit will impart His power into your life so you can be a witness to God and to what He has done through Jesus. You will change as you walk with Him, and people will see the difference in you. You will also get opportunities to share with others your experience since this change in your life took place; and it brings us into greater intimacy with our God too.

As we prepare to receive this gift, we should desire the giver as well as the gift (the in-filling). In so doing, we will receive.

33But seek first his kingdom and his righteousness, and all these things will be given to you as well. (Matthew 6:33)

This gift will embolden us for the work to which God has called us, which will be different for each of us as we are unique creations in God. Primarily, being witnesses to who He is and what He has done. Just as it began where the disciples were, (Jerusalem) – spreading to Judea, Samaria, the world, so it will be for us – starting wherever we are, and spreading out like the ripples on a pond.

SPEAKING IN TONGUES

4All of them were filled with the Holy Spirit and began to speak in other tongues as the Spirit enabled them. (Acts 2:4)

Speaking in tongues is a sign that you have been filled with God's Spirit, and everyone who is Spirit-filled has the ability to do this. However, I would like to point out that for those who have asked in faith for the baptism of the Holy Spirit, but haven't yet begun to speak in tongues, this is not an indication that they haven't received this baptism.

The gift of tongues is a language you receive from God, which you have not learnt and do not understand. But God knows its meaning, and it is the Holy Spirit in you, praying through you, and God uses it in a number of different ways.

Galatians chapter 3 tells us we receive this baptism by faith.

²I would like to learn just one thing from you: Did you receive the Spirit by the works of the law, or by believing what you heard?   (Galatians 3:2)

*⁵So again I ask, does God give you his Spirit and work miracles among you by the works of the law, or by your believing what you heard?
(Galatians 3:5)*

I believe that when you are filled by God, you will somehow know it, but do not desire this gift for an experience, or for the power that will come with it. This gift will enable you to have increased intimacy with God and will help you when you minister to others. The Holy Spirit, when He comes, brings with Him gifts. These gifts belong to Him and, even though they are deposited in us, they are still His and are to be used under His guidance. As we walk with God and grow in understanding and wisdom, the Holy Spirit will use us more and more by giving us insight into how, when and where to use the gifts.

God knows the desires of our hearts, what we need and when we need it, and I give here my own experience of receiving this baptism.

When I was born-again, it was only a matter of days later that I had the infilling of the Holy Spirit. I did not ask for this experience because I knew nothing of it, but I was very needy and God knew I was desirous in my heart for more of Him, and the Holy Spirit fell on me and filled me. I was on my own and didn't speak in tongues at that time because I didn't know anything about that either, until later, but knew it was a profound experience and it was of God. For the next two years I attended meetings and seminars, and always opted for those on the Holy Spirit because by then I understood I had received this baptism, and I was seeking speaking in tongues. When we were called forward at the end, I would always go. I was wanting to experience tongues, but it seemed to elude me.

Then a day came when I was so fed up with not having a break-through in this area, that I said to God that when the call came, I would go forward and I would listen to others speaking in tongues around about me, and I would copy them saying what I heard them say. It seemed like a plan! So at the end I went forward and followed through with listening, and as I opened my mouth to speak what I had heard, out came my own tongue. What happened?

I had not realised that God doesn't do this for us. He gives us our own individual tongue and, being the gentleman He is, doesn't force us to use it. We have to do the speaking – He will not speak for us. He gives us the ability – it is up to us to use it. So if you are having trouble getting started, take heart, and keep at it.

It is thought by some that this baptism, together with its gifts, ceased when the first disciples died. However, on the day of Pentecost (the day when the Holy Spirit came upon those waiting for this promise in Jerusalem), Peter went into the streets preaching about what had happened to

Jesus and why, and he said this:

> [38]Peter replied, "Repent and be baptized, every one of you, in the name of Jesus Christ for the forgiveness of your sins. And you will receive the gift of the Holy Spirit. [39]The promise is for you and your children and for all who are far off—for all whom the Lord our God will call." (Acts 2:38-39)

We see in verse 39 that this baptism, and all the giftings that are included in it, are for all of us, for we are the *far off* ones mentioned here.

If you desire more vibrancy, more of a relationship, more interaction and intimacy with God, in fact more of everything God has for you, then being filled with the Holy Spirit is the way forward. Don't just assume you have received the Holy Spirit's baptism – be sure. Don't miss out on His power in your life – we all need it!

WRAPPING IT UP

The word *baptism* comes from the Greek word *baptizo* and means – to dip (as in dye something); to immerse. So *baptism* in the New Testament always refers to saturation. We have looked at being baptised into the Body of Christ (totally, making us a new creation); into water (by immersion); and with the Holy Spirit (filled). In each case the experience is total.

Being baptised into the Body of Christ comes because you

have surrendered to Jesus and made Him your Lord, which allows the sacrifice of His blood to cover you, thus redeeming you from sin.

Baptism in water is total immersion in water – not a sprinkling – and confirms that you have changed into a new person through Jesus. It is like a funeral, symbolising the burying of your old self and emerging as your new self, and completes your separation from your old life into the new.

The baptism of the Holy Spirit – or being filled with the Holy Spirit – is an outpouring of the Spirit's power into your life, to give you the ability to live this new life through the power of God.

At this point I would like to clarify how the Holy Spirit works here. He is freely roaming the earth, drawing people to God through Jesus. At the moment of being born-again, He baptises us into the Body of Christ. Our new spirit is where God now lives.

When we are filled with the Spirit, this brings the Spirit's power, which helps us live this new life. This in-filling doesn't go into our spirit because our spirit is already made new and perfect and needs nothing further.

So, where does the infilling take place? It goes into our soulish part – the area we are to renew by the Word of God. When we are distracted by sin or with worldly things – thereby taking our attention off God – we no longer access this power in fullness.

> ¹⁸*Do not get drunk on wine, which leads to debauchery. Instead, be filled with the Spirit,* (Ephesians 5:18)

The New Testament was written in Greek, and the verb used here *be filled* is in the continuous tense, meaning we need to go on asking to be filled, because we can lose our focus on spiritual things, and thereby become less effective. Continuing to be filled keeps us overflowing and focused on the things of God. We need to ensure we stay topped up with this power in order to live our lives to the optimum.

The baptism into the body of Christ (being born-again) is done in the secret place. You may have been born-again in a public meeting, but the exchange of your old self into your new self takes place inside you.

Water baptism should be a public occasion – you are proclaiming your new life not only to family, friends and neighbours, but also to the spiritual beings that surround us which we cannot see.

Baptism with the Holy Spirit is also a public thing – it is the empowerment of your new self to live to God and minister to people. This experience can happen anywhere, and may take place when you are on your own, but the presence of God's Spirit will be seen by others as you become emboldened to speak out.

The more we focus on Christ, the more mature we will become, and the more we will stay full of Him. As we learn more about Jesus, our soul will agree more with our spirit, and two out of three means a life of victory in Christ.

Seek the giver, not only the gift – all else will follow.

Chapter 6

The Jewish Wedding

You may already know that in the Bible God gives everyday, natural pictures of things, to help us understand spiritual matters. For example, when Jesus was teaching, He used parables, and often referred to everyday illustrations like farming or fishing in order to make His point. Once we are born-again, we have the ability to begin to understand spiritual things on a spiritual level. However, before Jesus went to the cross and was resurrected, people could not understand spiritual matters in a spiritual way because they were not yet regenerated into the new birth – hence the need for natural examples to help us. Even after we are born-again, it is often helpful to see the natural picture to aid our understanding.

Over the years, traditions in life have built up or are changed with time. At this point I would like to take a look at the Jewish wedding as it was in Jesus' day, as it has a lot to tell us about what happened in the past, and what will come in the future.

THE BACKGROUND

We discovered in Chapter 1 that when a man and woman marry, they become united as one flesh, complimenting each other, with the same purpose but with different functions. Marriage was therefore, God's idea. He thought it up and instituted it.

Biblical marriage was in two parts. The first was the betrothal (equivalent of today's engagement), and was a legally binding contract between the parties. To dissolve it would mean a divorce between the two, even though the couple were not yet living together. The second part was the actual consummation of the marriage.

Here in the UK, we set a date for a wedding and everything takes place on that day. In some parts of the world weddings span more time than just one day. However, back in Bible times they took the best part of a week.

A wedding was an alliance between two families, negotiated and agreed by the parents, but not forced on the couple. It was an important event, involving the whole community, and the decision was often taken when the couple were quite young.

It is not known how old Mary was when she was betrothed to Joseph, but it is estimated that she may have been 15 when she became a mother. Joseph is thought to have been a little older.

The two families would negotiate the arrangements and discuss the bride price. Then the offer of marriage would take place. The bride price would be given by the father of the groom to the father of the bride. Upon the marriage, the bride would leave her home and live with her in-laws, thus, they were gaining an additional member of the family, but the bride's family was losing a member. The bride price compensated her family for that loss.

At the time of the betrothal it was celebrated, and the agreement between the two was reinforced by their drinking a cup of wine together, indicating the binding nature of the contract between them. The wine represented a blood covenant, which made the betrothal binding.

Following the celebration, the young man would tell his beloved that he was going to prepare a place for her and return for her once it was ready. He would then go back to his father's house to begin work on living quarters for the newlyweds upon their marriage. The young man's father would ensure the new extension was done properly, and would not allow his son to collect his bride until all was completed to his satisfaction, so in effect, the groom's father was the only one who knew when the right time to collect the bride would be.

In the western world today, our equivalent of the bride price would be a dowry, which is an amount of money or property which the bride brings to the marriage, although modern society doesn't tend to do this so much today. However, this practice of paying a bride price does still form part of today's culture in some parts of the world. I once had a student from Scandinavia who married a lady from Africa, and he needed to provide a bride price before he received her father's permission for them to marry – but back to our Jewish wedding.

Meanwhile, as the consummation of the wedding would not happen until the groom's father was satisfied that all was in place and the time was right to collect the bride, she would make and keep herself ready, knowing that there would be no notice of the groom's return. He could appear at any time, day or night. So, in order to be ready when he came for her, the bride kept the things she would need for her wedding easily accessible at all times. Her bridesmaids would also be on alert, and would also be ready.

Once the groom had the go-ahead from his father, he would take his friends with him and head for the bride's house, and on the way they would blow the ram's horn (the shofar) to let her know he was coming, and they would escort her and her wedding party back to his father's house.

Upon arriving at the father's house, the wedding celebrations would begin. The couple would enter into the room built by the groom, for a 7-day honeymoon. The groom's best friend would be waiting outside for the proof that the wedding was consummated; that is, the blood shed by the bride on the bed linen. This is important because it not only symbolised the purity of the bride, but also reinforced the covenant made between the couple. A blood covenant is the most binding kind of covenant.

The wedding celebrations would begin, and the friends and family of the couple celebrated for seven days. Then the couple emerged from their honeymoon.

THE CHURCH AGE

There have been different ages throughout history, and the one in which we now live is called the *church age*. It could not begin until Jesus had risen from the dead and caused the disciples to be born-again.

In each age, God deals with His people differently, so what distinguishes this, the church age, from any other in history? The main difference is that, although the earth has been in a terrible mess since the beginning, with mankind needing rescue, the answer to our problems had arrived in the form of Jesus. He is the answer to every question and every problem that has arisen since the dawn of time.

Jesus came to fulfil the law of Moses – He was the only person who could – and in so doing He achieved the way back to God that we needed. He took our sins, our sickness and disease, our poverty and lack in every area, our bondage in whatever form it came, and He nailed them all to the cross of crucifixion in His body. This selfless act by Jesus can set us free and, if we press in and take advantage of it, we can benefit from every aspect of it.

> [10]*The thief comes only to steal and kill and destroy; I have come that they may have life, and have it to the full. (John 10:10)*

Here Jesus is speaking. The first part of this verse tells us how Satan works, and what he did in the Garden of Eden – he stole our heritage by lying. Lying, stealing, killing and destroying are what he does, and he hasn't changed. He continues to steal from us the good things of God whenever he can. However, the last part of the verse tells us what Jesus came to do, which was to give us life in all its fullness. How do we get it? Through being born-again.

Why did He do it? Because He considered us worth it!

The benefits we receive from belonging to God through Jesus are wrapped up in the term *grace*. Grace is what God gives us (free, gratis and for nothing), and all we have to do is receive it. We cannot earn it, merit it, or deserve it.

It is a gift and it is FREE.

Our God is a God of mercy and grace. His mercy means He does **not** give us what we deserve for our sin (death – separation from Him); and grace means He gives us what we **don't** deserve (forgiveness and a way back to Him). God's grace is free, but in order to have His grace, we need to receive it.

This church age has been running for almost 2,000 years and will shortly come to a close, and there are comparisons between the traditional Jewish wedding with the end of this age. Let's take a look at these.

THE COMING WEDDING

The Wedding Alliance

This is the agreement between the young man and his prospective bride. He came to where she lived to seek her hand in marriage.

In the Bible, Jesus is often referred to as the bridegroom, and He came to earth to take back the authority over the earth lost by Adam, and to seek a bride – a bride He could spend eternity with.

This bride will be made up of men and women who are born-again and are ready and waiting for Him. Yes, even the men will be part of the bride of Christ.

The Cup of Wine

The young woman had the option of accepting or rejecting this man. If she accepted him, it was reflected in the drinking of a cup of wine together to signify she belonged to him. This equates to mankind who all have the opportunity to receive or reject Jesus as Saviour and Lord.

Once the two young people have agreed to marry, they are betrothed – today we would say we were engaged. The difference between their betrothal and our engagement is that their betrothal was a binding agreement between the two. It was a covenant between them. Covenants were usually sealed by the shedding of blood, and this marriage would be sealed with blood on the wedding night. But for now, it was confirmed by drinking wine.

The wine at the betrothal corresponds to the wine taken at the communion service, sometimes referred to as the Lord's supper, the Mass or Eucharist, which is symbolic of the blood shed on the cross for our sins. If we accept Jesus and become born-again, then Jesus' shed blood is ours. Those who do not accept Jesus, and are not born-again, have no claim on His blood.

> [20]*In the same way, after the supper he took the cup, saying, "This cup is the new covenant in my blood, which is poured out for you."* (Luke 22:20)
>
> [28]*"This is my blood of the covenant, which is poured out for many for the forgiveness of sins."* (Matthew 26:28)

Here Jesus was using the cup of wine at the last supper, just before He went to the cross, as a picture of His blood, the shedding of which would bring us forgiveness. He was on the brink of crucifixion and resurrection, which would usher in the new covenant.

The Bride Price

The father of the groom gave the bride price to the father of the bride. It was negotiated between the families.

There is a bride price that has been paid for the heavenly bride – this bride price was not negotiated, but was the most valuable thing the Heavenly Father could give – it was His Son. The price paid for the Bride of Christ was Jesus Himself when He bled and died on the cross.

The Groom Prepares a Place

Once our couple have entered into this covenant (confirmed at the betrothal by the drinking of wine) and once the celebrating was over, the promised groom got ready to leave. He must return to his father's house and prepare a place to bring his bride. Jesus, who came to earth to seek a bride, told his disciples:

> *²My Father's house has many rooms; if that were not so, would I have told you that I am going there to prepare a place for you? (John 14:2)*

Jesus stayed on earth for 40 days after His resurrection before ascending to His Father in heaven to prepare a place for His bride, before coming back to claim her.

The Timing of the Wedding

In our background account we found that the groom returned to his father's house in order to prepare the accommodation for the couple upon their marriage. He knew it would take a while, but he didn't know how long. He was also aware that he would not return for his bride until his father was satisfied that everything was in place.

As we have seen above, Jesus has returned to His Father to prepare a place for His bride, and it is only the Father who knows the exact moment when Jesus will return. But until that time, we need to be ready, because He will come at any time, without notice.

The Groom Returns

Once everything was ready, the bridegroom's father would send his son to fetch the bride. Although the bride was unaware of the groom's return, she would hear the ram's horn (shofar) being blown to herald his arrival.

At Jesus' return for His bride, those who are ready and waiting for Him, will hear a trumpet. He will arrive at a time we do not know and we must be ready.

> *[16]For the Lord himself will come down from heaven, with a loud command, with the voice of the archangel and with the trumpet call of God, and the dead in Christ will rise first.*
> *(1 Thessalonians 4:16)*

At various times since Jesus' day, the church has thought that He would return for them. They were disappointed. So, how do we know that it will not be long now? The Bible is full of prophecies about Jesus' return, and the things which needed to take place before He could come. Of all these prophecies, there are now only a few left to be fulfilled, and as a result we should be watchful. He will come at a time when most people do not expect Him.

7 Days of Rejoicing

God's ways are not our ways. His thoughts are not like our thoughts. He sees and understands things differently from us. He even looks at time in His own way.

> *[8]"For my thoughts are not your thoughts, neither are your ways my ways," declares the LORD.*
> *(Isaiah 55:8)*

The seven days of rejoicing which took place at our Jewish wedding equate to seven years for the wedding to come. It's going to be quite a party! The bride will be with Jesus in heaven for seven years before He returns to take back the authority over the earth that He won on the cross.

The Wedding to Come

No matter what happens in the world, or what we experience on a personal level, we have a great hope for the future. Just as our young betrothed couple looked forward to their wedding day when all the preparations had been made, they would come together with joy.

Jesus came to find a bride for Himself. We have looked at the fact that born-again ladies are also sons, and that born-again men will be part of the Bride of Christ. Jesus will return for His bride at the right moment, sent by the Father, and we will be taken to be with Him forever.

> [17]*After that, we who are still alive and are left will be caught up together with them in the clouds to meet the Lord in the air. And so we will be with the Lord forever. (1 Thessalonians 4:17)*

This being *caught up* is a reference to what the church call 'the rapture', when we will leave this earth and go to be with Jesus forever.

He will come back soon for those who belong to Him. Those who are not looking for Him will not hear the trumpet. Are you ready?

PART 3

Chapter 7

On Your Marks!

Anyone who has ever participated in a race will know that we are called right at the start to be ready for the off. I wonder if I have stirred you up by what I have included in this book. Let's take a quick look at where you are at right now, and whether you are ready or not for change, challenge and commitment.

We all need to change and grow, we all need to be challenged, and probably most of us need to be more committed to our walk with God. In fact, we are all at different stages in our faith journey. If you have already been born-again, then you will understand how you fit into what I speak of next. For everyone else, the rest of this chapter is the culmination of all I have included in this book.

DO YOU QUALIFY?

When it comes to God and His Kingdom, things often seem up-side-down. This is true if you look at them through worldly eyes. However, the things of God are actually the right-side-up.

You may have heard the following saying by Mark Batterson:

> *GOD DOESN'T CALL THE QUALIFIED*
> *HE QUALIFIES THE CALLED.*

If you haven't yet made Jesus your Lord, maybe you don't feel you are qualified – why should you? There are examples in the Bible of people who definitely didn't feel qualified to walk with God and serve Him. Here are three of them.

- o Moses – who committed murder before he was commissioned by God to lead the Hebrews slaves out of Egypt; and,

- Gideon – who came from the weakest clan in his tribe, and he considered himself the least in his family, yet was called to lead the nation of Israel.

- Also, St Paul – prior to his Damascus Road experience, he persecuted Christians, pursuing them, throwing them into prison, and condoning their deaths, and afterwards referred to himself as the worst of sinners.

God has called others too, and there are many, and that includes you and me, and we have all *done our own thing, walked our own way* and, basically, *got it wrong*.

We may not think we are worthy – and indeed we are not – but remember, unworthy we may be, but in God's eyes we are worth rescuing. If God accepts Moses, a murderer, Gideon with no confidence, and Paul, a persecutor and murderer, there is no barrier to anyone, no matter who they are or what they have done or not done.

Take a look at 1 Corinthians 1:27:

> *[27]But God chose the foolish things of the world to shame the wise; God chose the weak things of the world to shame the strong. (1 Corinthians 1:27)*

If you didn't feel qualified before, surely this verse applies to you. It certainly applies to me. I was cast aside by my husband having experienced a damaging marriage, breaking my spirit and leaving me to bring up two young children on my own, with no means of support and zero self-confidence. I identify as one of the *foolish and weak things* mentioned above. I certainly felt that way. Does this also apply to you?

Subsequently I discovered that God was there for me, and He has taken hold of me and made me what I am today.

> *²Do not conform to the pattern of this world, but be transformed by the renewing of your mind. Then you will be able to test and approve what God's will is—his good, pleasing and perfect will. (Romans 12:2)*

I laid hold of God, by being born-again and filled with His Spirit, and I have renewed my mind through His Word. He has taken me from being nothing, to knowing who I am in Him – as a son and a co-heir with Jesus, and part of His bride.

You can do the same. Will you do it? It is a simple matter, and will change your life, but it needs to come from your heart.

> *¹³You will seek me and find me when you seek me with all your heart. (Jeremiah 29:13)*

We discovered that our heart and our mouth must be in agreement for the following verse to be effective. Remember we said that just praying a pray will not gain us anything – this step must be an action from your heart. You may wish to refer back to *DECISIONS, DECISIONS!* in chapter 1.

⁹If you declare with your mouth, "Jesus is Lord," and believe in your heart that God raised him from the dead, you will be saved. (Romans 10:9)

Faith which saves us from our sins will come from our heart; it will not just be something we think, it will be part of us. Saving faith coming from our heart can transform our sinful life into a life of righteousness. Up to this point we have been in rebellion against God. Being born-again is us renouncing our act of rebellion against Him – in fact, putting up the white flag of surrender.

If you have reached the point of wishing to make Jesus, Messiah and Lord of your life, then you will need to come to Him in prayer, and you may wish to use the following:

> Lord Jesus, I come to you as I am, knowing I have sinned and fallen short. Thank you for your sacrifice on the cross in my place, and for freely forgiving all my sins. I give myself to you today and ask you to be my Saviour and Lord, and I receive this new life in you by faith right now.
>
> Amen

Welcome to your new family. If you sincerely meant this prayer then you have now become a child of God.

A NEW YOU

So, what can you expect if you prayed this prayer, and meant it from your heart? The Bible says you have been changed.

> [17]Therefore, if anyone is in Christ, the new creation has come: The old has gone, the new is here! (2 Corinthians 5:17)

The Passion Translation of the Bible puts it like this:

> [17]Now, if anyone is enfolded into Christ, he has become an entirely new person. All that is related to the old order has vanished. Behold, everything is fresh and new. (2 Corinthians 5:17) (TPT)

If you have prayed this prayer (or a similar one) and meant it from your heart, one of the three parts of your being (your spirit) is now changed; your spirit is now born-again; you have been adopted into God's family and become a son of God, and part of the bride of Christ, whether you are male or female.

This is the beginning of your journey into life with Him. From now on, pursue God and the things of God. Be baptised in water, and seek your purpose in His Kingdom. You will be rewarded with satisfaction that will not fade. A wonderful future awaits those who belong to our God and are waiting for the return of Jesus.

GOING FORWARD

Just as Jesus and the disciples needed God's help, you too will need help with this new life, and I encourage you to pursue the baptism of the Holy Spirit. Here are some more words you may wish to use.

> Father, I thank you for Jesus and His sacrifice, and acknowledge I am now a new creation both through and in Him. I ask for the baptism of Your Holy Spirit to help me live this new life, and I receive Him in faith now, and thank you for all your provision.
>
> Amen

EPILOGUE

Much to my astonishment, I have enjoyed writing this, my first book. I hope you have enjoyed reading it. If, by this point, you are born-again, you will discover the new creation you have become by following the steps outlined here. But whether this is all new to you, or you have walked with Jesus for a while, I hope this book has somehow challenged you, and stirred up the things of God within you, and given you a deeper understanding about what happens when you become a Christian. We now know that we have been made in the likeness of Jesus, and my prayer is that you will be changed more and more into His image as you look forward to a great future in and with Him.

I will end with the following verse of scripture, which God gave me for each one of you.

> ^{13}*May the God of hope fill you with all joy and peace as you trust in him, so that you may overflow with hope by the power of the Holy Spirit. (Romans 15:13)*

ABOUT THE AUTHOR

Jennie has been connected with church throughout her life, and has been a born-again Christian for the past forty years. She responded to God's call to go deeper into her understanding of her faith some years ago, which led her to attend Bible College from which she graduated in 2015. As a child and young adult, she desired to be a teacher, but life got in the way and led her down another path. However, while at Bible College, the call to teach emerged once more in a strong way.

Following graduation, she has spent her time teaching, discipling and mentoring, and has now written her first book. Her aim is to share her faith in a simple, clear fashion, with the goal of opening up what can seem complicated and obscure, to a wider audience.

Wisdom of Faith

M I N I S T R I E S

We are a passionate team of trainers, teachers, speakers, mentors and life coaches who specialise in helping people to discover their unique hidden gifts required for their success.

The highest purpose of every human is to live, to discover, how to give whatever is needed to achieve a community that exists for the benefit of all life.

We contribute toward this by training people to find and fulfil their Inherent Life Purpose.

Wisdom of Faith Ministries - My Inherent Life Purpose Matters
For more information on our training and events please visit:
www.wisdomoffaithministies.com

To locate further Books To Bless *books:*

- Enter the ISBN number of **THIS** book into the Amazon Search Bar.
- Select book – the Book Title and Details will appear.
- Below the **Book Title** you will see links to **Author** & **Contributor**.
- Click on **Jennie Papa** (Author) to see further books when available.
- Click on **Books To Bless** (Contributor) to see <u>all</u> books published.

ISBN:9798799731588

ENJOYED THIS BOOK?

If this book has been helpful, I shall be grateful if you will spend a few moments posting a review on Amazon. This will bring it to the attention of others wishing to increase their understanding of their own journey into Christianity.

Thank you

Below are two books from the **Art That Speaks** collection. (Art by Rita Clark.) To see more books in this ministry's range, please click on **Books To Bless (Contributor)** as stated above.

ISBN: 0798566010268
(UK SPELLING)

ISBN: 0798741026267
(UK SPELLING)

"The LORD bless you and keep you;
The LORD make his face shine on you and be
gracious to you;
The LORD turn his face toward you
and give you peace."'

Numbers 6:24-26)

Printed in Great Britain
by Amazon

75431928R00070